Sweet Home

First published in 2025 by the Indigenous Literacy Foundation
Gadigal Country
Level 17, 207 Kent Street
Sydney NSW 2000
ilf.org.au

Cataloguing-in-Publication details are available from the National Library of Australia

www.trove.nla.gov.au

ISBN 9781922592972

Design and Typesetting by Steven Dunbar
Printed by Opus Group

SWEET HOME

Stories of Country and family

By Students from Ḏawurr Boarding

Illustrated by Daydae Yunupingu

This collection is dedicated to Stuart Martin,

who is the glue that connects us all together.

Contents

Introduction

"I'm proud of them."

Stu, perhaps more than most, has reason to be proud of the group of students who wrote the stories that make up this collection. Stu is a Rembarrnga man from Bulman. He has worked with the students at Ḏawurr Boarding for four years. He is their family connected through kinship and has been instrumental to the success they see at school. We talked together to write the introduction to this book.

Ḏawurr sits on Rirratjingu Land on Yolŋu Country in Nhulunbuy, East Arnhem Land. The boarding school is home to Indigenous students from across the Northern Territory, who come from their communities to study at Nhulunbuy High School. Ḏawurr is the Yolŋu word for honeybee. When Rirratjingu Elder Witiyana Marika gave the boarding house its name, he told the story of the mother bee who works and helps the small offspring from the hive when they go out into world. She teaches them wisdom and knowledge.

This is what Stu has to say about it:

"Ḏawurr to me – when I first started – I didn't know the meaning of it until family started telling me stories. I saw the names of the kids and it was just like home. Since I walked in the door, it got me, you know, straight away. Ḏawurr to me, it's a really big name. You know the honeybee? Old Man was saying that the honey is there. The honeybee always flies out but always comes home. It's just like the kids. They fly and then they come back home. It's their home away from home. And it's a special place to me."

Students come to Ḏawurr from diverse communities, sometimes hundreds of kilometres from each other. They speak Dalabon, Mawng, Rembarrnga, Kunwinjku, Kriol, Yolŋu Matha (Gupapuyngu, Djambarrpuyngu, Dhuwaya and Dhuwala), Murrinh-patha and more. But once they get to Ḏawurr, they quickly learn how they are all connected to one another. As Stu explains, all the mobs here are connected to each other somehow, and it is his job to help the students learn this story:

"My role with them is about relationships. Most of the kids are related to me anyway. Even when I walk at the school, all the kids, even the local kids, they know who I am. I'm glad I can touch them that way. I keep telling them to not give up and to keep going. I'm an important person to the kids here. I have a different connection with them. It's very strong. It doesn't matter if they come from this way or that, I become that person who connects them all together and helps them to find how they are connected to each other. I help them understand who they are. It's really important to the kids and to me."

This book was conceived as part of a literacy program we run at Ḏawurr. Students spend Monday afternoons working on their English language skills and after a long day at school – often learning in their second, third, fourth or fifth language – these additional hours are a huge ask.

We decided one day that it would be good to anchor these lessons in something tangible and quite quickly settled on an ambitious idea: together, we would write a book. We needed a theme and decided that all the stories should focus on the idea of 'home'.

Home is a particularly important and complicated concept in the lives of many of the students here. As Stu explains: "Home is where the heart is. But home is two things for the kids. It's home, and then it's home away from home. It's always good for them to be thinking about home but they do get homesick. With the kids, they're always thinking about their homes. But they also know that they have two homes. I think we make them feel that way."

With home in mind the students spent many afternoons generating ideas. They thought deeply about the meaning of the word and carefully planned a story inspired by their reflections. Most of the stories came together over many months of drafting and revising.

The process was used not simply as a creative exercise but as part of a teaching program, where students learned the skills of speaking, writing, reading and proofreading at a level that met their needs. It's important that the stories are read in this context. To a monolingual English speaker, some of them may read as works-in-progress. But we hope that readers read each student's story slowly and listen to their words deeply. All of them have important things to say.

Ultimately, the book exists for the students themselves. It is a testament to their hard work and something that their families should be incredibly proud of.

The students who authored the stories appear in this collection noted by their initials.

We hope that these stories help readers understand a bit more what home looks like for young people in the remote Northern Territory. Most importantly, we hope that these stories bring readers joy and laughter.

Stuart Martin and Oliver Friedmann

Students come to Dawurr from Communities across the Northern Territory. They have been highlighted on this map.

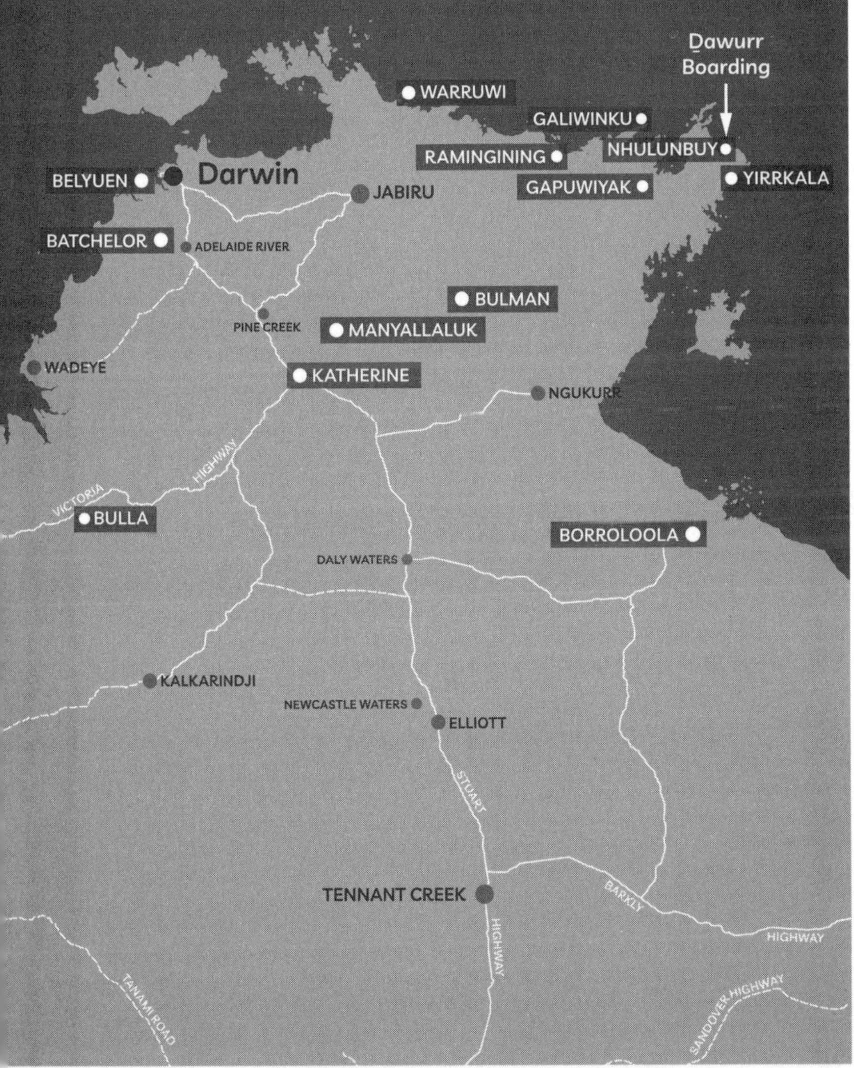

Batchelor, My Sweet Home

HN, 12, Batchelor

I remember when I went fishing at White Stone. White Stone is a place in Batchelor in the Northern Territory not far from where I live. It looks like a mountain rocky form and has a little creek to go fishing and swimming. To get there we have to drive in the car. We mostly go fishing because there are crocodiles in there. The creek always looks black and dark, the perfect conditions for crocodiles to hide.

It was my first time being there with my little brother. My little brother was six years old. He is often a troublemaker and does not behave, but I was so excited to finally visit this place with him. He loves hunting and fishing, and we were both using handlines and sometimes little rods. This was a special moment for us because it was my first time there and my brother and I are close. I was the good luck charm for the family as we caught lots of fish.

It's a bit hard for them to catch fish there. Once, I caught six bream in one day, the most I had ever caught. We were using bullocky beef as bait. This was from a recent time we had hunted a bullocky. Sometimes we save some bullocky for the dogs, sometimes we use it for bait, other times we put it in bags and freeze it and when we need it for dinner we can get it out. Other times, we make beef jerky out of it. My uncle makes the best beef jerky.

I have caught and seen lots of animals and creatures there. One time I caught a yabby. Another time I saw a goanna in the water with something in its mouth. I think it was a bug or something. I remember that one time when I was fishing, I saw a big croc. It was so big that it was almost as big as my nan's car tyres. As we were looking at it, it just decided to go under the water never to be seen again. I think it moved on from there.

Then the next day I caught a big turtle on my handline, it was hurting my hand and I was struggling to pull it up. I pulled it up all by myself. I knew it was a turtle as it was pulling slowly at first, because it has webbed feet, and it was trying to swim away. But as soon as someone pulls the line it swims faster as it is scared. It was the size of a laptop and it was so heavy. It was a short-neck turtle.

My family was so excited that I caught this turtle. But they were most excited about eating it. We love turtle. To eat it, you first need to bust the side open and take all the guts out of it. But leave some in, the good bits, like the heart and kidneys. We put alfoil in its guts, make sure the puss has stopped coming out and then put it on the fire. We know it's cooked when we hear that hissing sound. Then we wait for one to two minutes after.

We get a hammer and hit it from the middle and keep hitting it until the shell is broken. You have to watch out for the bladder bag, it's no good to eat. My favourite part of the turtle is its long belly bit. I also love eating the head and legs. If you put salt on it, it tastes delicious but without salt it tastes plain. It is tough meat, you've gotta pull at it to eat it, it does not melt away in the mouth. With all the remains, we put them in the fire and let them burn and return to the earth.

We go hunting for bullocky, not far from home, past the pub, and out into the bush. If you want to hunt the bullocky you have to make sure you know where the wind direction is going. You must wait for the wind to be coming from the bullocky towards you to make sure that they don't sniff you. We then hide behind a tree and sneak up on it and then shoot it. We separate the meat, some for the dogs, the head and the bum. The rib bones for us, these are my favourite bits. We take all the legs and the back strap as well. When we cook it, I love putting salt and BBQ sauce on it. Smoking the buffalo is the best.

My last story of hunting is about pig hunting. I remember one time when my uncle was hunting for pigs. I was little then. I was scared and I didn't know what to do. My uncle said, "Get the rifle, get the rifle!" I instead got the knife and almost dropped it on my foot. I was that scared.

My uncle came over and grabbed the rifle and shot it before it charged me. We always have the knife with us to make sure that they don't charge us, so we can protect ourselves.

This is my story, what's your story? I encourage all young Australians to tell their story because no matter your age, your story matters.

There The Grass Is Always a Soft Green

BM, 14, Belyuen

I'm in Nhulunbuy, a long way away from home. I'm here with other people from different places and we're here to learn.

When I am back home, I am in Belyuen. Belyuen is one hour's drive from Darwin in the Northern Territory. My house is white and it has three bedrooms. I live with my mum, great granddad, two brothers, uncle and aunty. We have a rooster named Ducky. I sleep with my mum and my two brothers, Trent and Tytus. In our room, we have a big TV, a PlayStation 5, a laptop to watch movies and AC to cool us.

I go camping at Two Fella Creek. There we hunt for crabs, stingray and turtle eggs. There is a beach and on the other side is a billabong. We have a handline with beef on it and throw it in the billabong. We leave it for the day and hope to catch a turtle. One day I caught a long-neck turtle. We twist the turtle's neck and cut the throat. We then throw it on the fire. We eat the back legs, the front flippers and the throat.

The throat tastes so good. It has a similar taste to goanna, which has a similar taste to fishy chicken.

I play rugby league with my brother, cousins and uncle in my backyard. There the grass is always a soft green. It smells fresh. The sprinkler is always on, that's why the grass is green at the backyard.

One time I was playing rugby with my brothers, cousin and uncle. As I was running towards them to try and score a try, my brother tried to tackle me, but I did a spin move and dodged him. While I was still spinning, my cousin was running straight at me. I bumped him by accident and knocked him out. When he got up, he was seeing things and bleeding from his nose.

We play all afternoon. We don't usually count the score because we're just playing it for fun. We play until we're exhausted. After we finish playing, we stumble into the kitchen for some Zooper Doopers from the freezer to cool us down. When I eat Zooper Doopers it hypes me up. It also gives me a brain freeze.

We play on the trampoline. The water from the sprinkler makes the trampoline bouncier. BowWow and I take it in turns to flip forwards and backwards. I like jumping on the trampoline

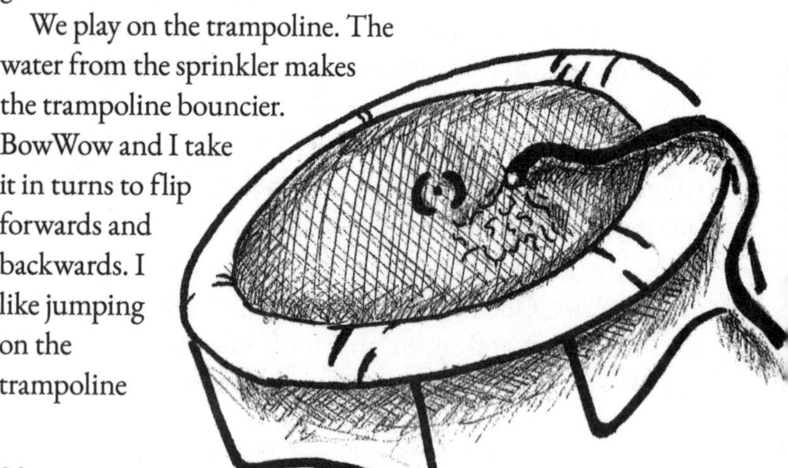

because you can do all sorts of tricks. When you are doing a back flip or front flip it feels like you are floating. Your body twists, your feet bend and your hair hangs. Your legs get tired. Your stomach feels like turning upside down. As I flip, water sprays my clothes.

When I am home, I also love playing basketball with family and friends from the community at the sport and rec centre. It's a huge indoor green basketball court. We always do crazy stuff like dunking on players, shooting crazy tricks and crossing each other. I always spend time with Tytus and Trent playing hide 'n' seek. We also play a tag game at the oval.

Sport is fun because you can come up with new games. It makes me happy because it's all about having fun and playing with your family and friends.

Homelands

SH, 14, Borroloola

I remember when I was nine years old. I went to a station called Brunette Downs, between Barkly Homestead and Borroloola, close to the Northern Territory and Queensland border. My mum, sister, brother and I loaded into the Landcruiser GXL and drove along the red dusty track from Corella Creek for about three hours. Road tripping with my family is fun and it can also bring us all together. We listen to country music, one of my favourite songs is 'Thinkin' Bout Me' by Morgan Wallen. Exceedingly long road trips can make you very sleepy.

As soon as we drove in, we went down a muddy dirt road and a couple minutes after, we looked up at the tree and saw a goanna way at the top. We all jumped out of the car and started to get a suitable number of rocks to throw at it for dinner. We all race to find the biggest rocks to hit it first. My brother was shooting at it while I was climbing up the tree. I grabbed the goanna by its tail and slinged it down on the ground. We all rushed in and started holding it down to hit it over the head.

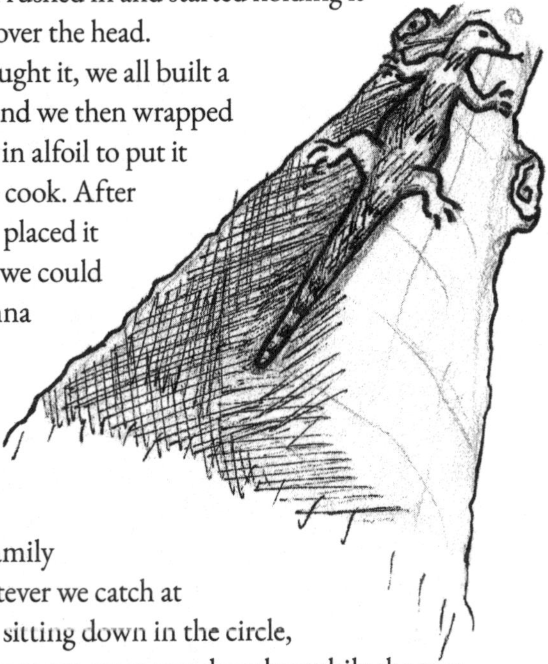

After we caught it, we all built a fire, gutted it and we then wrapped the goanna up in alfoil to put it over the fire to cook. After we cooked it, I placed it on the mat, so we could all share. Goanna is everyone's favourite. It makes me happy when we come together as a family and share whatever we catch at hunting. I was sitting down in the circle, and I looked up at my great grandmother while she was telling us a story about Jesus and the religion days. She told us one of the stories how Jesus took Peter, James and John, the brother of James, up on a high mountain by themselves. While they watched, Jesus' appearance was changed his face became bright like the sun, and his clothes became white as light. Then Moses and Elijah appeared to them, talking with Jesus. Peter said to Jesus, "Lord, it is good that we are here. If you want, I will put up three tents here one for you, one for Moses, and one for Elijah." There's another verse that says Honor your father and your mother, that your days may be long upon the land which the Lord your God is giving you. You shall not kill. You shall not commit adultery. You shall not steal. You shall not bear false witness against your neighbour. You shall not covet your neighbour's house. You shall not covet your neighbour's wife, his male or female slave, his ox or donkey, or anything that belongs to your neighbour.

I live in a remote community called Borroloola in the Northern Territory. There are no schools nearby, so I must fly all the way to Nhulunbuy to boarding school. When I am at boarding school and away from family I get homesick and miss them every day. I do get to call my family, but sometimes take it out on staff at boarding because I want to go home.

I have a close bond with my grandmother because she grew me up at the age of five. She teaches me our language, the traditional ways and cultures about our past. She also teaches me how to dance and teaches our family members when they are going through law. I sit with my grandmother and first she challenges me to see what she is saying in Waanyi Garawa language. She said to me "Budangku nana kirriya naj-kany yarrambaja," which means "women are not allowed to watch the man do corroboree/dance" and I said in return, "Burrurri daba nangka, jukuli-i, barrku-u." Which means "men used to fight with boomerangs."

It is difficult to remember what she is saying to me, and it makes me feel like I do not know what I am doing. But she is understanding and patient. She makes me feel like happy, safe and it makes me trust her. I am sitting in front of her on her bed. Her bed color was white, soft, comfortable, and around me was walls full of paintings that my dad painted. He painted the history of our family. The paintings are all sort of sizes, and some may have dot paintings of animals. He uses black, red, white, grey, and brown to paint the animals. He does this so we know our history and where we come from. The place that I am from is called Nicholson River. It is a place owned by the Waanyi people. At Nicholson we have sacred sites. At home we have a little community called Murrunmarula. That's the place where I grew up at when I was younger. Sometimes when we are bored, we go swimming at two waterholes called Big Rockhole and Little Rockhole. That's my favorite place to go fishing, we catch a lot of different fish.

Sometimes we play a little game called Indian Cowboy. It starts off with any numbered players. We all get four, three, two or any number of cards each. We must use up the cards to make ten. So, if one card is in middle and you have two cards in your hand you must make ten with the card in middle and your two cards. My grandmother is the best at playing the game because she taught us to play.

My grandfather's brother is a hunter, he goes and hunts for emus, cow (bulligies) and kangaroos.

I have fond memories going hunting with him and my friends. He makes it fun because we get to run and chase the kangaroo, goanna, and emu. My grandfather is always the one that shoots the gun, it freaks me out because I worry about hurting another person.

Sometimes when my mum, sister and brother have nothing to do, we like to go fishing. Our favourite fishing spot is a big freshwater creek. We use both handlines and spears, only the boys will use the spears. The best time to catch the fish is at nighttime when it is quiet and the fish come out, we catch a good number of barramundis which I like to cook up and eat. Sometimes we also go fishing on my aunty's boat when we have not caught any fish at the creek.

Sometimes I drive the boat because I enjoy it. We fish with rods and handlines to catch fish. Being on the boat in ocean makes me feel comfortable, happy, and relaxed. Sometimes we do competitions to see who can catch the biggest fish. When they do they get the biggest prize. We do all sorts of competitions like Easter, Christmas, and Halloween.

Through my life experiences I want to pass this message on to you. Family comes first, having adventures together and doing what you like. So always remember that your parents are the reason you are alive and happy.

Bulla Days: A Slice of Life From the Top End

KRL, 14, Bulla

I grew up in Darwin in Moulden but then we moved to Bulla. It's dry but when we get rain the bridge gets so full that we can swim and if you go down a bit you can fish. You can sleep in all day in Bulla. It's near Timber Creek and the bridge connects to the Timber boat ramp. It can be boring in Bulla because there is nothing to do but there's heaps to do when we go to Kununurra for shopping for food, clothes and for family.

Sometimes all we do is sit down and play Call of Duty Mobile or PlayStation. Sometimes we go out to play with little brother and the little family. Last time we visited WA was last year and that was for the football carnival. I played for Palmerston and the only team we lost to was Haileybury. When we first got there, we went to a Korean place to eat dinner. After that we went to the local oval. We played a little bit of football. Then after dinner we went to the rodeo grounds. We slept there for three nights and stayed there for four days.

I like it when I go for fresh killer (beef).

How we get the beef is we run it over and, when it is under the car, we have to hit it with an axe. I'm happy when we kill it because we get to eat. It dies and then we skin it. When you skin a cow you start from the head and work your way down. You leave the legs when you skin it because you can't eat them. There's too much bone in that area. Sometimes, if you want, you can cut the tongue off too, but you can't cut from the front of the mouth. You have to go from around the throat area where the tongue connects with the throat. I learnt how to skin from uncles and dads.

I like the rib bone. The way we cook the rib bone is we grab tin foil. We put salt on the bones and then wrap it around in aluminum foil and make sure it's all covered. Then we put it on the fire and we don't wait until the outsides brown, we wait until it's black. We rip the skin off and then we eat it.

The last time I went to go get fresh beef was when I was 13. There was me, Tristan, my two little sisters, four or five uncles, two brothers and my mum and dad. We went to the station and killed it at the place the cattle rests. Me and Tristan stayed in our car but everyone else got out. While me and Tristan were sitting on the front of the car, there was another bulliki looking at Tristan funny.

Tristan tried chasing it but then Mum growled at him.

The way they killed it is they had that axe. They didn't hit it with the sharp bit, they hit it with the dull part. The first hit it didn't die but became really weak. The second time we hit it really hard to make sure it was dead. We tied the rope over the bulliki's neck and took it to cut it up. We turned around and started driving to Bulla. We put all the meat in the deep freezer. First thing we cooked was the rib bone and the rump. Rib bones are for a snack. Rump is for dinner.

My Cousin-Brother, Tristan

NRL, 12, Bulla

This is a funny story about my cousin-brother, Tristan. Last year in Bulla, my mum, dad, and other little siblings decided to go out fishing. Tristan, Kallem, Tristan's older sister, Tana, and I did not want to go fishing, so Mum told us to stay at our daughter Rita's house.

We were bored at Rita's house, so we went to the park for a few minutes. We then went back to our own house, got some of the snacks that Mum had told us not to eat and took them back to Rita's house! By then we were laughing and talking with each other. The sun was setting, and the rest

of my family was still not back yet, so we collected some firewood for Rita to make a fire.

We sat on the verandah while Rita told us stories about Jesus. She eventually went inside, which gave us a chance to make some tea and coffee with lots of sugar. We went crazy!

Rita came back outside to stand with us under the verandah cover. The fire was still going, with all of the lights on inside and outside the house. All of a sudden, all the electricity in Bulla went off! Tristan got scared and he ran and jumped over the fire just to stand next to our daughter.

A couple of minutes later, Mum, Dad and everyone else came back. We told them about Tristan getting scared and they all laughed! A few minutes later the power came back on, and we all went to bed. What a day!

Out Hunting With the Family

TN, 12, Bulla

I grew up in Bulla. It is near Timber Creek in the Northern Territory. It is dry place and it has lots of trees. I live with my mum, dad, sister and brother. In Bulla, we play tip and we run around with our friends and family.

I like sleeping in a lot. But I also enjoy going swimming under the bridge in Bulla, near the roads. It is a very tall bridge. We jump into the river from the bridge. After that we walk back home in the heat and it helps to dry off.

I've got lots of stories to share of my times out hunting with the family. This is my favorite thing to do in and around Bulla as I get to spend time out bush, time with my family and we get food for everyone.

In hunting season, we go to the junction to hunt cows and duck. I go there with my uncle in his car. Kellum, my cousin, comes hunting too. We use a car with a bull bar to chase down the cows. We run over them to kill them. We hit their skull with hammers. We skin them up and after that we chop them up. We put the pieces of meat in the back of the car on a tarp. We leave the rest of the cow there for the birds and dingoes to eat.

We love to eat the heart of the cow. We boil it in water with salt and vegetables to make a stew. Everyone loves to eat it. The leftovers go to the dogs.

I remember when dry season came in Bulla, one day we were out hunting cows. My uncle's brother got chased by a massive cow. He was trying to scare the cow away. But that cow kept coming towards him, faster and faster. My uncle, he had to run fast to get away. He ended up throwing sticks at it to make it go away but it only made it angrier. Cows look very scary when they are angry! My uncle got away from this cow by climbing out of the pen, but he almost got hit by it. We ended up killing the cow as my uncle ran into the pen which made it easier for us to capture. It was a good ending, my uncle's brother was bait.

When we would hunt ducks, we would go out carrying car spanners as this was the only thing we had in the car. We don't own any rifles, so we had to get clever. When we spotted a duck we would sneak up on it and throw the spanner at the duck. You had to have a good aim and a powerful throw to hit it and knock it out. When we hit one, we'd grab it, pluck the feathers, skin it and take it home. We cook the ducks by boiling them up and serving them with vegetables and adding a little bit of seasoning to it. It tastes delicious.

My family's fishing spot is near Bulla, close to a station. We must drive there as it's slightly too far to walk. The river we fish on has a pump that pumps up the dirty water, the clean water goes into the houses and the dirty water back into the dam. The river is lined with trees and bushes and has lots of shade for us to sit underneath. We don't swim there as there are crocodiles. I've only seen the skin of them on top of the water. But we know that they are there watching our every step. My sister, mum, dad, nanas, little niece and I, us mob we all go fishing here. One time we caught a barra. A giant one. It was our lucky day as soon after I caught a turtle. But after that my little niece was rolling around, rolling back and forwards. We were confused why she was constantly rolling. Then, all of a sudden, we saw a massive snake under the sheet that she was laying on. My big sister grabbed her daughter, my little niece, and we all ran. The snake slithered away into the river. No one got hurt we just let it do its thing.

Definitely our lucky day.

I'm Out Here Trying to Do My Best and Spread Kindness

CA, 17, Bulman

I did so many violent things when I was younger that I almost got suspended from school. I was sitting in a chair facing the principal because I got into a fight with one of the other students. We were discussing my behaviour and my short temper because this was not the first time that this had happened. I was going to get expelled. I was feeling a bit dizzy because this would have been my first time getting expelled from school. But my sister begged for another chance and the teacher gave me one.

I remembered playing in a playground when one of the kids threw something at me. So,

I got angry and started punching his face. It ended up in a disaster. Parents had to come up to the school and then a big argument started down the street. After that, parents started swearing and fighting for their kid's sake until one of the kids owned up because they started the fight first. Then our parents stopped and apologised to each other.

Everything went back to normal the next day we went back to school. Me and the other kids shook hands and started playing football again. I have learnt that violence isn't the way to solve problems. Now I'm out here trying to do my best and spread kindness.

This story is about me and my country. Bulman is a small community in the Northern Territory, with lots of big things like fishing place and fresh water. When I'm home I like to go out fishing, hunting, swimming, camping and learning about country. It's fun because I like spending time with my family and friends. My family and friends are important to me. My mum likes to cook. She likes to cook all sorts of meals like chicken curry, homemade pizza, beef with vegetables and much more.

My brother, Junior, likes to play Call of Duty Mobile (CODM) with me every Friday afternoon because I really enjoy playing with him. He's good at playing CODM. He even beat me a couple of times. Sometimes, when I win against him, he gets angry and tries to beat me up, although I can't feel a thing because he's a kid after all. Me and my sister don't really get along that well because when we were little, I used to bully her a little bit all the time. Now that I'm older I feel bad about it and wish we had a better relationship.

Bulman school for me was like a safe zone because all the teachers were so kind and helpful, however, when I was younger, I was bullied so many times because I was little. But I always got back up.

When I was in primary school, me and the other kids, we used to look up to the middle years, coz back then we thought they were really cool. They were big, doing all these like cool things, going around places. One time they went to Sydney for an excursion. It made us feel like they were showing leadership.

We used to play this game called populicious bully. All the seniors would chase us and grab us and put us in a cage. We teased them, they chased us. The teachers joined in as well.

In Bulman we keep busy doing lots of things. We go on top of a hill next to our house and get bush gum. It's sort of like a tree sap. It tastes really good. We play footy at the oval with friends.

I moved schools to Nhulunbuy where I board. I'm away from my family which made me feel a bit worried at first if I was going to make friends. But I do have my friends BowWow, Lyndon and Deshaun who I grew up with since childhood.

The Story of Brother and the Big Buffalo

DN, 18, Bulman

The horn is big and sharp. When I first painted it, it was beautiful. The paint was black, red and orange. I picked those colours because they represent my culture. But now it's getting old and rusty. It is in my grandmother's outstation, outside near the panel gate close to a big white bark tree. My grandfather, he tied the buffalo horn up on the panel and leant it near the tree. I was probably about 14 or 15 years old when he put it there. It's been there since.

My brother and I went to an outstation in his tray on the back of his Toyota Landcruiser – that's my grandmother's country. He told me that he was going to leave me next to a billabong, while he went out to go to a big open plain to look for wild turkey. But he couldn't find any. He went back to the outstation. I waited for him for three or four hours. Luckily, I had a shot gun. I got up and started to walk back from the billabong to the outstation.

Then I heard an animal breathing heavily and I heard some

bushes moving really fast. I saw this big black buffalo and it was running at me. Luckily, I stopped him by shooting him in the face. I went up to the dead buffalo. Well, I thought it was dead, but it was only wounded. When I realised it was still alive, I felt scared. I know I was scared because my heart was beating that fast. It got up and charged at me. But I had run out of bullets and he was still standing. He was moving more slowly but still running up to me, so I ran. I just put the gun next to a tree and took a big sprint. Then, I heard a car bashing through the bushes.

I just kept running and running. Soon, I heard the sound of a 308 again. It sounded like a firecracker exploding. I stopped and turned around. I saw the car on top of the buffalo and my brother was close by with the gun in his hands. He shot it three times in the head. I filmed it all on my phone. In the video you can't see much because the phone was shaking too much.

I was dead serious and pretty scared. But then my brother came over and started laughing and I started laughing too. We cut up the buffalo and put the pieces into the car.

We drove home. He was talking about the buffalo all the way there. He was talking about how big it was and how sharp the tips of its horns were. I was sleeping but I was still listening a bit.

My brother is a mentor. He talks about things with me and when I get in bad situations, he comes to me and has a good yarn. He makes me feel good all the time. He's a very good brother to have.

Once we had dropped the meat we went back again and got

the skull. When we got back home we left it for two or three months. And then I painted it. My brother went and got all the paints for me. I didn't want to paint it, but he forced me.

"If you paint this you can use my car for anything", he said. The car is a red Toyota Landcruiser. It's got emu springs on it and mud tires. He was dead serious.

I finished it and he gave me the car keys. So now I can use it any time I go back home.

The horns of that buffalo still sit on the fence. When I go back home and see them, it reminds me of the day that it chased me.

I Couldn't Stop the Smile Spreading Across My Face

LL,15, Bulman

I live in Bulman, Northern Territory. I also used to live in Belyuen and Manyallaluk. My house in Bulman has stairs up to the house.

I remember I was lying in bed and my dad told me that we were going hunting. I couldn't stop the smile spreading across my face. Hunting makes me happy because I am with my family. We all loaded our white Nissan with camping and hunting gear. I slid the spear under the dusty seat of the troopy.

Dad makes hunting really fun because he lets me shoot the gun and drive the car. The day we were chased by a pig, we were busy looking at ducks in the swamp and I saw the pig standing in the mud behind a bush. We chased it first and then Dad shot it with a shotgun from about five metres away. The pig then turned around and growled at us and my dogs. Then the pig ran away.

We turned and ran to the car. I jumped onto the bonnet, then up on top of the car. It was bumpy on the top but I felt safe because everyone was in the car. I was on the roof for one minute before I got down and got in the car. We then drove back to the outstation.

Another time, I went to Kununurra with Clontarf on an AFL trip. Clontarf is run by Ricky and Bernie. We go on trips with them. They also do fun stuff and make us do pushups. Bernie and Ricky teach us a lesson for swearing.

On the return trip from Kununurra to Nhulunbuy we stopped in Bulman to do a walk with the Rangers. I also did this walk with my uncle, brother and cousin and Lee Gordon (teacher from my school). We walked part of the way to Gorpulyul and were lucky enough to take a helicopter ride for the rest of the trip. I could see my outstation. The pilot took us down the valley to see the water. The walk was fun and we had barramundi for breakfast.

My brother's dad caught the barramundi and my little brother speared a small barramundi. They got these in a little creek crossing.

We went to the waterfall and showed Lee Gordon the rock art that is there. The rock art is of lollypop men, drawn by the Mimis. While we were there we saw a little croc too. We were gonna kill it, but we didn't.

Family and Fishing

TL, 16, Bulman

James was driving us to the wharf. I was in the front seat pumping some music. The whole gang was digging it. The boys were dancing and singing along with Morgan Wallen's 'Thinkin' Bout Me'. I remember the leaves were flying everywhere, like a cyclone. We got out of the car and Daydae went to the end of the wharf and he began to catch snags.

The wharf was windy and it was so boring because we weren't catching anything. I was sitting at the end of the wharf with my mate Deshaun. The air smelt like fish, and I could taste the salt. I looked at Deshaun flicking the lure into the water, and it reminded me of a time when Deshaun was swinging a lure and got hooked in his hand.

Deshaun was swinging the lure and it swung back towards him. He tried to block his face, but he got hooked in his hand. If he hadn't had blocked his face, the hooks would've landed in his eyes. Deshaun took it like a man. We had to take him to the hospital. The nurse took the hook out and cleaned it up. He had to have a week out of the water, which meant no fishing.

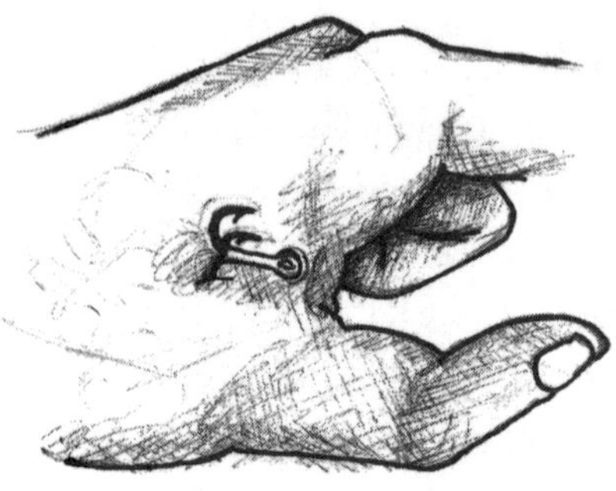

On that day, it was kinda scary because I don't like seeing people get hooked in the hand. I think I have a phobia of deep cuts. It makes me feel like shivering, like when you bite your teeth together and you get goosebumps.

Deshaun and I are close. His mum grew me up. She is my nana. She is kind, she always buys me stuff. I used to stay with them, and Deshaun used to walk me to school. When kids teased me, he was always there for me. We always laughed together and played games.

Good friends look after each other. Care for each other. They fight and can still be best friends. We have never fought before, just play fights. This is what makes our friendship so fun.

My home where I live is Bulman. I live with my mum, dad, grandfather and baby sister, Ava. When I'm there, I fish at this one fishing spot called Manjine. Manjine is a famous fishing spot for barra. You can also catch bream and turtles there. Manjine is a beautiful river that we drive to from Bulman for fishing because the water is blue and clear and you can see lots of wildlife swimming. There is water in the river all year round and the birds sing. When the wind pushes past the trees it makes lots of squeaking noises. I go here with my uncle, my brothers and my cousins. Sometimes Deshaun comes too.

To catch the barra we use live bait. We catch the live bait on hooks. Sometimes we use soft plastics to catch the barra. To catch turtles, we also use live bait, but we need to leave it a long time in the water.

We make a homemade oven to the cook the barra. We dig a hole, put hot coals in it and then put the barra in the hole. We cover it with leaves or if there is an old roof tin, we put that on top. We wait for it to cook. Once it is cooked, we take all the leaves or tin off, peel the skin off the barra and eat it. Sometimes I make a barra sandwich with salad!

When we catch a turtle, we twist its neck and break its spine. Then we cut its throat to clean the guts. We pull them out to clean the turtle. We use the turtle guts to catch red claw in the yabby pot. After that we bury the turtle in hot coals and wait for it to cook. Once it is cooked, we crack the shell with a hammer or anything that is hard. We eat the legs and neck. The liver is the best part, it tastes the best.

We go hunting at a lighthouse at Cox's Peninsula. When we go there, we catch mud crab, barra and mangrove jack. My favourite is mangrove jack. At the lighthouse there is a croc with oysters stuck to its back. Lots and lots of them. My uncle stepped on it one day and saw its head. The croc is really big.

Some of the most important things to me in this story

are family and fishing. There are lots of people who are important to me, but the most important are my mum, dad, Unksy Deshaun, my baby sister and grandmother. Deshaun because he is funny, my baby sister because I love her and she's cute. My grandmother because she cooks me really good food. She cooks the best lasagna.

We Go Night Fishing Down By the River Next to the Homeland

TH, 14, Bulman

When I think of home, I think of walking around, playing with friends going to the oval, shooting some birds with a slingshot. Bulman is a quiet place. Sometimes I live in an outstation, sometimes in town. The outstation is called Beggetti, where my family sometimes go camping. We go fishing, swimming and hunting. It's not far from Bulman, a 15-minute drive. We go there every Friday and stay for the weekend. We go there because our family passed away there. It's important that we go back there to look after the land for our family. Baggetti has three houses, we stay in them. They have cool air conditioners but only when we put on the generator. Every night we go night fishing with spears and rods and fishing lines. We go night fishing down by the river next to the homeland. We catch barra, sharks, sword fish, catfish and turtles. There are a lot of crocs there.

Beggetti has a swimming pool there. A tank with a shade over it. It's so deep and cold there. We go swimming there in the afternoon when it gets hot.

I play footy sometimes for the Bulman Buffalos. All my uncles play for Bulman Buffalos and my grandpa. I feel proud to be in the team and am excited when I run onto the field. When I get the ball, I go for the first option: a short 45. My favorite is a check side. When we win we feel happy and excited and do flips on the field. And we chant: "GO THE MIGHTY BUFFALOS."

Sometimes me and my friends go hunting for ducks, kangaroos, pigs, cows and turkey with our dogs and we go a long way in the bush in our Toyota far away from Bulman. We always come back late to Bulman, around 1 am, cook what we hunted and share it with the families. I love NT bush turkey – you know those big birds the bustards. If we get a big one, it will feed the whole family. We pluck its feathers and just put it straight on the fire, to fry it up. First on the flames then on those hot ashes. Serve it with salt and pepper and some soy sauce, arrr I cannot wait to have some again.

I miss going hunting and fishing with family. When I go back for holidays this is the first thing I will be doing.

I only moved to D̲awurr Boarding school in Nhulunbuy at the end of Term 2, 2024. This is my first time up here. I was a little bit nervous but mostly excited because I had lots of friends and family from Bulman attend D̲awurr before me. I have still been able to play lots of footy. Every Wednesday and Friday morning we have Clontarf footy training and sometimes after school. I thought I would try out for the Michael Long Cup team where I had to go along to a training session. The coaches put us through drills and we played a mini game. I breezed through the training session with a smile on my face and a love for footy in my eyes. Footy runs in my family. My older brother plays for Nightcliff Tigers. My other brother, he has lots of trophies in his house all from playing footy. I want to be like them and play footy. I am now one step closer as I found out at the start of August 2024 that I got selected for the Michael Long Cup team to play for the NT Thunders. I will be heading to Darwin to play soon. I cannot wait. Me and one other fella from the school are going. It's going to be a great time true.

I am excited for what is to come.

Gurrumuru, Darwin, Elcho Island

RRW, 13, Galiwinku

I grew up in Gurrumuru until I was six years old. My family and I then moved to Nhulunbuy because my grandmother and my grandfather passed away and we wanted to be closer to family. I was happy about our move to Nhulunbuy because Dad was working there and I didn't get to see him a lot. Gurrumuru is a community that is a two-hour drive to Nhulunbuy, East Arnhem Land.

From when I lived in Gurrumuru, my favourite memories are of fishing with my family. My mum, my sisters, Dianne and Kaitlin, and my brothers, Kane and Cliff, and I would go fishing to the same saltwater creek. We would go down to the local creek and fish. The creek is a 15-minute drive from home. Sometimes we would all walk there, which would take 40 minutes to get there. We caught catfish, barra, stingray and turtle. We use a handline with a baited hook to catch a barra and catfish.

I remember one day when we were walking back home

from fishing with my cousins we saw buffalos. There were three babies and a mum and a dad. They started chasing us. We ran up to the trees and climbed up them to get away. After trying to scare them by yelling at them, they went away and we got down and went home. When we got home, we cooked the catfish and the barra on the fire. After we cooked the fish, we went swimming at a freshwater river called Wirrmunga and then we went home. When we go fishing we have to be careful of the crocodile, so we stand far away from the water.

We then moved to Darwin because Mum got a job there, but we didn't stay long because we couldn't get a house. So, we moved to Elcho Island. In Darwin, me and my sister went to the beach one day, we didn't know that it was a nude beach. It was scary and funny.

I also moved to Elcho Island as my mum got a job painting houses. We stayed for three months and then we left. I didn't like living there. There are naughty kids there.

It was fun moving to different places. I met lots of new people and made lots of new friends.

Now, I live in Nhulunbuy. A couple of months ago, James, Daydae and I were going fishing at the wharf. James was driving the troopy on the road next to the quarry when a kangaroo jumped out and ran into the side of the car. Daydae and I were happy and excited and asked James to turn around.

We saw he had a broken leg, so Daydae dragged the kangaroo to the side of the road. James took out the tyre iron and we told him where to hit it to kill it. James then wacked him on the back of the neck and put him in the back of the car. We took him to James' house to pick up knives. When we were there, we showed Henry, Matilda and Eddie and told them what we were going to do with it. Daydae promised to save Henry some tail to eat but we ended up eating it all.

We used a machete to carve the skin of the kangaroo. Bokeem and his dad taught me how carve a kangaroo like that. We kept the legs, ribs, liver, tail and spine. The best part of the kangaroo is the back part. You can boil it or cook in frying pan.

I Take Care of My Dad and He Takes Care of Me, and Together We Take Care of My Mother

MM, 15, Gapuwiyak

I remember when I was ten years old, my grandmother taught me to be a kind Christian. She told me about God's stories. I keep understanding it more every time I see her. I ask her for more stories of God and she always takes her bible out and reads for me.

My favourite story from the bible is about Noah. I like Noah because he brings all of the animals on the ark, he talks to them and saves them from the flood. Noah built a big ark because God told him a big flood was coming. He walked to the village and told the people to join him, but no one listened. Noah, his wife, his son and daughter helped him to build the ark. When the ark was ready, God told him the flood was about to arrive, so Noah got two of each animal to save them from the big flood. All the people were yelling at Noah to help them from the big flood. Noah said them, "You don't believe in God." The meaning I take from this story is to trust in God. I try to trust in God and listen to his story.

I miss my grandmother so, so much. I miss her love and her kindness. I was so happy when she visited me at boarding. She reminds me of Gapuwiyak and the life I have there.

I like my country called Gapuwiyak and I miss my school back at Gaps. My dad told me about our culture and about my totem. When I reached five years old we held a ceremony to choose a totem. My elders chose my totem, and it was painted on my belly when I had my first ceremony. My totem is a shark. My skin name is Balangi. My last name is Mununggurr. My dad also told me how to dance.

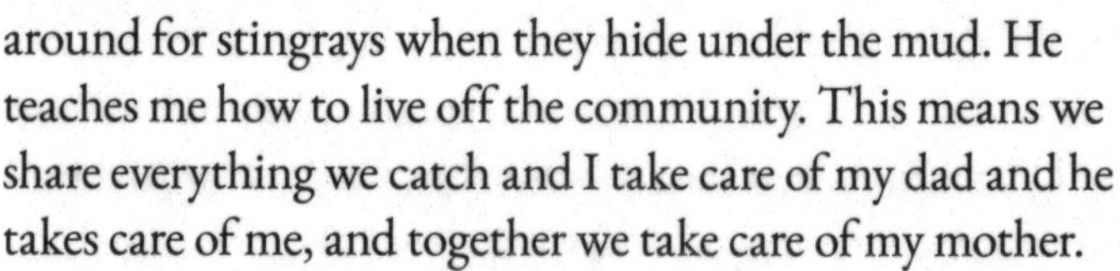

My dad always takes me to country called Wandawuy and he tells me how to hunt for kangaroo with the spear and how to look around for stingrays when they hide under the mud. He teaches me how to live off the community. This means we share everything we catch and I take care of my dad and he takes care of me, and together we take care of my mother.

I like my mum because she is a good cook. She always makes chicken curry, and she also makes beef and pizza. These are all my favourite foods. And after that she brings me some snacks, like Skittles and Oreos. She bakes chocolate chip cookies. She will take me fishing to get some saltwater barramundi for eating. She will bring some fruit, snacks and drinks for us to share while we're fishing. My mum uses a fishing rod and I use a spear. Mum always catches more fish and I catch more big mud crabs.

When I walk up to someone and when I ask them something and they try and tell me something that I don't believe is good for me, I will always call out to my mum. I trust my mum because she tells the truth. She has a lot of mates that look after me.

Once, I went to Balma with my family. We went to go fishing and spend a weekend there. When we got there, my father told me to come fishing with him in the morning at 5 am. I went to sleep and then my papa woke me up from a big dream and he told me to grab all the lures and spears so we would be ready to go. Then, my papa grabbed the keys, and we headed off to go fishing.

When we got the fishing spot, he told me to go grab my rod and then he told me to put bait on it and chuck it into the river. After that I was feeling bites from a big barramundi. I felt one swallow the big bait, so I pulled the rod real hard. But the fish dragged me closer and closer to the water. He pulled me into the water and my dad ran to get the rod out of my hand. The fish pulled again, and my dad moved backwards and pulled the rod at the same time. He got the fish. We packed up all our stuff and hopped in the car. We returned to where we were camping. My mum grabbed the fish, and my dad collected some wood. My dad made a bonfire. In my family I also have two siblings, an older sister and a younger brother. When I spend time with family I feel happy and they take care of me. I feel protected by all my sisters and brothers and by my grandmother and by my mum and dad.

Me and My Family Went to Daly River

AD, 14, Katherine

In the holidays, me and my family went to Daly River, Northern Territory. It took us nearly three hours from our home in Katherine. On our way we stopped at Pine Creek to have a break and had something to eat. After that, we had to get back on the road.

We entered the Daly Region and passed a creek. Mum said pull up because she wanted to stretch her legs. My dad got a handline and wanted to throw it in the water. Once it was in the water, he left the handline there and took me and my little brother Chad to the shallow part of the creek just to dip our head in because it was hot.

We were driving past a place called Tipperary where Mum told us she used to go to school and stay when she was young. She said that when she was in school, she stole her teacher's cake. The teacher growled at her and hit her with a ruler.

When we got to Daly River we stayed with my cousin-sister, Beatrice, and her grandson, Neil. At her house, she had a pet cockatoo and a black fluffy rabbit. The rabbit had a big patch on his side because one time my nephew went and ripped its hair out.

At one point, my cousin shouted out to Neil.

"Go clean upstairs you lazy idiot."

Then we heard the cockatoo say the same thing. We all started laughing.

After that, we had food again and started getting ready to go out fishing. We went with two cars, out to the big saltwater river. When we got down to the river, me and Neil was taking turns throwing the fishing net off the bridge. We got lots of live bait and put them in a bucket full of water and took it to Mum and Beatrice. Mum used the live bait and caught a medium sized shark on a handline. My dad caught a barra on his rod. We kept the barra and stored it away in the fridge. It was about a metre and a half.

Then us kids went swimming under the bridge. Further upstream, I saw Mum struggling to pull something in. That's when Orlando, my big brother, went and helped her. It was a bull shark and Mum cut a bit off and left the rest up on the bank. We went back up top to the house to have food and cook the shark with damper and rice for dinner. It was yummy.

We all wanted to go night fishing. So, we did. My dad shone the torch at the rest of the bull shark that Mum had caught. He found two glowing eyes. He then jumped in the car and put the big bright lights on and found a big croc eating the shark on the bank.

The next day we went out bush to my sister's block to pick up some hunting gear. We got a shotgun and a cross bow. After that we went out to a place called Goose Hole and there we went hunting. My big sister's son shot three geese. We then went to the little river, and we went swimming. My sister let me, Neil, my big brother and Sheyanne have a turn with the shotgun. We were shooting this glass bottle.

"First one to knock the bottle down gets to have first piece of the goose."

It was so powerful when I pressed it. I got flown back from the shotgun and missed the bottle. Even Sheyanne and Neil got knock back and missed. But my big brother hit the bottle only because he knows how to hunt and shoot.

The sun was slowly setting, and we started to head back to Daly River. When we got to my sister's house, we made a fire to cook the goose. When me, Neil and my little brother were getting wood, my little brother saw a snake.

"Nake nake there look Neesha!" he yelled.

I looked down and found a big brown snake. I picked up my brother and ran back to my sister's house. Then she took us with the car to go look for wood. When we were driving back a big buffalo ran in front of the car. My sister was panicking because she nearly hit it. She pulled a sharp brake and then she turned to the side of the road to check if we were alright. Yes, we were okay, so we got back on the road and headed back to Daly River.

The next morning Mum and Dad took us kids looking for mangoes in the trees around Daly. The mangoes there weren't ripe, so we went out to the mango farm where there is always a lot of mangoes trees with big and small mangoes. We all got like two full bags each!

Family is important to me because family is mostly who you need around you to make you feel okay when your upset or feeling down. I like spending time with my family because they can teach me things I don't know.

In the Hills We Saw Waterfalls

SD, 16, Katherine

In the holidays me, Mum, Dad, my sister, Neesha, and little cousin-brother, Chad, went to Bulla for one week of fishing. My big brother Orlando got in trouble and so had to stay home to look after the house. Mum and Dad was preparing for a long time to go out bush as a family.

We was heading out but Dad forgot his fishing rod. Mum and Dad was arguing about the rod because Mum wanted to keep going but Dad wanted his rod. So, we had to turn the car around just to go get the rod. We got the rod and was heading out of Katherine.

"Bye, Katherine, see you next time," Chad said as we passed the train bridge.

"We are only coming back in one week." I laughed.

We left Katherine about 2 pm in the afternoon and got there about 7 pm at night. When we was driving, we passed a blue tree that someone painted. We also saw a donkey in the middle of the road. Dad pulled over but the donkey was just looking at Dad and Dad was beeping the horn for the donkey to move. Dad tried to drive but the donkey ran in front of our car, so he pressed his foot on the brakes hard. We leaned forward. It was scary. Then we got to Victoria River. In the hills we saw waterfalls. It was so beautiful.

When we arrived my Jarbuch (mum's aunty) was waiting for us. When we jumped out of the car she gave us the biggest hug and kissed us on our foreheads. She told us to get some rest. We unpacked the car and my Jarbuch gave my mum and dad a spare room. We was sleeping with my Jarbuch in her room, me and Neesha and Chad. Chad didn't want to sleep with Mum and Dad, he wanted to sleep with us.

The next morning, we had breakfast before going to Timber Creek because my Jarbuch had to get some groceries for her house. When we was driving to Timber Creek we saw waterfalls and all the creeks were really full because it was wet season. I also saw a water goanna, but we just kept driving and went back to Bulla. Dad was fueling up so that we could go fishing. We went inside and helped my Jarbuch with her shopping and Chad wanted ice cream, so we bought him ice cream. Jarbuch told us to help her unpack the shopping.

We went down to the river with my cousins. Mum and Dad was meeting up with other family. We was swimming. I got bored of swimming so I asked mum if I could go fishing. She said okay, so me and Neesha and Chad went to the old bridge. We was fishing under the old bridge and I was teaching Chad to throw a line. Neesha brought Chad his chair to sit on and Chad was just playing with his line until he caught something. He sung out to me to help him. I ran to him and pulled the line back and he caught his first fish. It was a bream. Neesha caught a mullet and we was still fishing until the water started going fast.

Mum and Dad drove up and dropped off Mum. Mum was telling us that the river is coming up. Her thong got swept away in the water and my cousin's car was stuck at the place we were swimming at. The water was coming up fast, so Dad came and picked us up. We had to go back to the community to get help with my cousin's car. Our car is an automatic and my cousin's car was manual, so if Dad towed the car our car would've got a broken engine. But our family came and helped and we went back to camp and had shower.

I then asked Dad if I could have a test drive of the car. I drove to the airport and went around the rubbish dump and went back home. Mum was making lawa (damper) and we was eating it with fresh beef. It was so yummy! Then we had a chill night. My mum went to my aunty and they were talking stories all night. I went too because I just wanted to go and watch movies on her TV. My aunty and uncle was cooking more beef on the fire and I went back to my Jarbuch's house and went to sleep.

The next morning, I slept in and I could hear Mum getting up in the morning with Chad. They was going to my other dad's house (Dad's brother). They went for the morning and had tea and lawa and beef. They went to the highway looking for roadkill for bait. They brought back a kangaroo and we chopped that up and put the meat into the fridge and chucked the kangaroo body for the dogs. There were also pigs in the community.

Mum and Dad came back and our car had no fuel so we had to use our cousin's car to go Timber Creek to go and get fuel for our car but we had to push start our cousin's car because it was manual. We was at Timber creek, we got some bait and some food for the road. We jumped back into our cousin's car but then realised we had to push start it again. Luckily, we had family at the shop. We asked them to push start us. Then we was saying bye to them. We was on the road back to Bulla and got the fuel out of the car. Dad told me to help him fill our car up. It was so hot, but we knew rain was gonna come. My dad stayed home while me, Mum, Neesha and my other mum (Mum's sister) and Chad went down the river at Baptist Place for fishing. Mum drove down the hill. When we went there we was fishing and then a big dark cloud was on top of us. But it wasn't raining yet. My other mum caught a turtle and we was catching little catfish.

Mum got annoyed. She was making fire for the turtle and Neesha's line was pulling. She ran to the line and when she was pulling it back it almost pulled her in. But Mum ran and helped her pull her line back in. It was a big catfish. After that it started to sprinkle and the water was going muddy because the river was coming up so we packed up and jumped back into the car. Mum said I could drive so I jumped in the front. Mum was in the passenger seat. I drove up the hill and drove back to our Jarbuch's house and we got the fish out of the back. Mum was gutting it so we could put it in the deep freezer. We went next door to my other mum's house because Mum was there talking stories all night.

The next day we got up and got ready. We had breakfast

and went for a ride to the station and Dad gave me a test drive on the car. Then we went back to the house and was just having a chill day. Then we went out fishing at Lily Creek. There was a man fishing there when we went there. He was talking to my Jarburch and he gave her three barramundi and then he left and we went to the spot where he was fishing. We went fishing. Dad and Mum was fishing when I saw a live bait, so I caught it and put it on my line. I was fishing and then my line pulled.

I sang out to Dad so he could pull the line back. We caught a big barramundi. As Dad was pulling it back to the riverbank, the line came loose and the barramundi jumped back in the water. Luckily, my live bait was still on the hook and I threw my line back into the water and then the same barra pulled my line again. Dad pulled it again and we finally caught a good 80cm barramundi. I just got so excited because it was my first time catching a big barramundi.

The other mob was still fishing. I was in the back of the car putting the fish in the car. We was getting ready to pack up because the sun was going down and it was getting dark. When we got home, we started having showers just to get the dirt off us and my Jarbuch and Mum was cooking the other barramundis. My big barramundi was in the deep freezer.

The next day was our last day at Bulla because we had to go back for school. As we were getting ready to pack, our uncle brought a couple of fresh beefs to give us to take back to Katherine. We was putting our luggage in the car and our blankets, and just as we were jumping in the car our Jarbuch came out and hugged us and kissed us goodbye. She was praying for us to have a safe travel home.

As we was driving out we saw her crying, wiping her tears and waving at us. Then we was on the main highway travelling. We went pass Timber Creek, then Victoria River. We turned into a place called Campbell Springs and had a quick swim in the spring water. Mum and Dad was fishing again. Mum got a big short-neck turtle and Dad got two short-neck turtles. Chad got sick because of a hot soft drink. We rushed back to Katherine and unpacked and then rushed him to the hospital. Luckily, he got treated and we took him back home. Mum made him shower in bush medicine and after that he was feeling better.

We Were All So Excited to Finally Find Them Finches and Echidnas

GF, 13, Manyallaluk

This is a story about my community Manyallaluk. Manyallaluk is so small, there are roughly 27 houses and buildings. This includes the school. The community is surrounded by bush, with a river close by. We call that river Tourist River. We often go fishing and swimming there. I live in Manyallaluk with my mum, her name is Elena. She had three children. My oldest sister, Rickiesha, is 17 years old, and my youngest sister, Diandra, she is three years old. I love my sisters, especially my baby sister, we always play tip together.

Although I live in Manyallaluk now, I mostly grew up in Bulman which is a couple hours' drive from Manyallaluk. We moved from Bulman in 2019. When we moved it was just my mum and Rickiesha, Diandra was not born then. When we arrived, I started going to the school there. There were only 10 or 11 kids there and we were all primary school students. Rickiesha started going to Ḏawurr Boarding

School in Nhulunbuy. I missed her dearly when she started going to boarding school.

My old teacher, Ben, and his wife, Meg, they worked in Manyallaluk for maybe eight or nine years, from when I was in creche, and they are still working there now. They are the only teachers at the school. My mum and Dusty's mum, Keisha, work at the school as well helping in the classroom. One of my favourite activities at school was going out bush. One time we went out placing cameras in trees, in the hope to help find echidnas and Gouldian finches. To our luck the cameras caught some Gouldian finches on footage. We were all so excited to finally find them finches and echidnas. We only found one echidna though. This was a part of a school project where we were looking for them, to see if they were in the area, and then we learnt about them in class.

Five years after my sister went to Ḏawurr Boarding School, I started coming as well. This year, 2024, is my first year at the school. I was nervous to first come to school in Nhulunbuy, but my sister was there to help me out and get me ready for my first time up here. Now she is in Katherine. I still miss her dearly.

We're Gonna Get Killed From This Buffalo!

SL, 15, Manyallaluk

A black shadow sped through the thick scrub. I could hear my sister screaming.

"Guyu guyu buffalo."

With my heart pounding I ran and climbed up a tree. So did the others.

I remember when I was back in Bulman, me and my family went camping out on our country, Gopulyu outstation, about an hour drive from our house. There are three houses at the outstation where my family used to live before the big flood came and ruined the houses and the generator. The houses are near a big river, but the river is usually dry all year until the wet season arrives. That's when the river always fills up. Once there, we swim in the little creeks along the riverbed. We clean up the outstation and sit down talk stories all night and day.

Once we got there, we made our tents and went to go look for firewood. We like to look for a fallen white gum tree. We gather little and big logs. Then we put the little logs down, put paper in the middle and put the big logs on top of the paper. Then we burn it to get a fire started. We put the big logs on top of the little logs. This way, it will keep us warm when we're sitting by the fire talking stories all night.

The morning of the next day, we packed up the fishing line, baits and spare hooks to go on my father's country. When we got there, we started to walk upstream where the river had dried into small pools. This is where most of the turtles get blocked. We threw our lines in the water and waited for the turtles to bite.

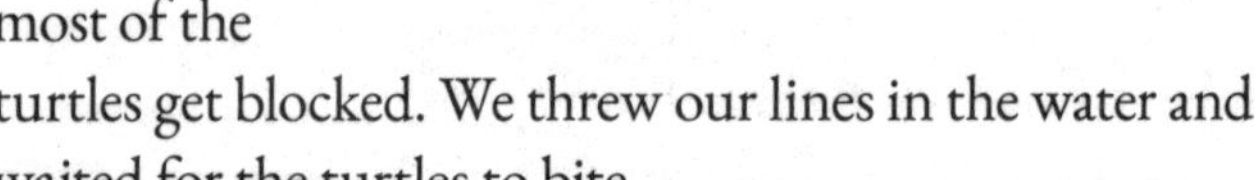

It is different to catching fish because fish just take the bait and go, but turtles take a bit longer because they must swallow the bait slowly. When we bring a turtle on the bank, we grab it by the neck and try take the hook out. If the turtle has swallowed the hook, we cut the line and put on another hook. My sister and my mum usually kill the turtles. They grab hold of their necks, tip their heads back and cut the throat until we see a white string. Then it's dead.

The sun was setting so, after we caught about ten turtles, we started to pack our fishing line and hooks and walked back to the Nissan. My sister put the ten turtles in the back of the car in a crate. We left them alive because we didn't want to kill them yet. We were worried they would rot. They stayed completely still and in their shells.

My brother-in-law tried to start the Nissan, but it wouldn't start so we had to push start it. But it still wouldn't start. My mother knew a short cut road to get back to the outstation. It was getting dark, so we started to walk. We decided to take two of the turtles with us walking. I was carrying them because the other kids were too scared to hold them.

Everyone was starting to get very frustrated and a little scared because that was me and my sister's first time back at our father's country. We were worried that our grandmothers and grandfathers were going to call out for us to follow them into the bush so they can take us away. When my grandparents passed, their spirits went back to their country, which is also my father's country. Whenever me and my sisters would go to their country, we'd often hear them cry from the other side of the river. My mum and dad tell me that it's dangerous to stay around the river when the sun is setting because they'll come and make our ears so deaf that we can't hear anything or anyone. Then they'll make us walk far away into their cave where they'll keep us forever.

It was while we were walking through the bush that my sister saw a huge buffalo running through the trees. It was all panic. I didn't know where it was running from but could hear it. I ran and climbed up a tree.

"Jujie!" my mother yelled. "Get down and burn the fire you dopey idiot before we're gonna get killed from this buffalo!"

I was very tired when I ran up the tree and forgot that I had the lighter in my pocket. I had to get down, run and get the dry grass. I burnt a dry pandanus tree. After the buffalo ran away, we walked until we got to the billabong. We instantly knew we were nearly at the outstation, and we could see the road tracks. My sister and my brother-in-law walked back to the camp with their son, and my other big sister and brother-in-law stayed with us because we were too tired and cold to walk back.

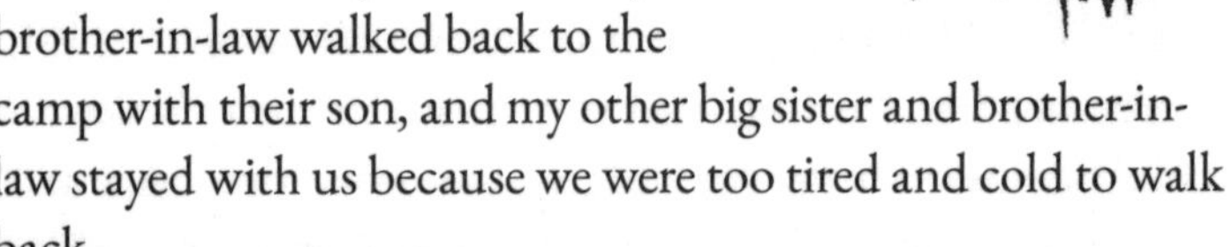

By then it was too dark and cold, so we went and gathered a lot of firewood and made two big fires. Luckily me and my nephew brought two blankets. I shared my blanket with my two nieces, and my nephew shared his blanket with his two cousins and his grandmother. My sister and her husband didn't go to sleep because they kept putting woods on the fire so it wouldn't die out. The next morning, we woke up and started to walk back to camp. My sister and her husband made breakfast for us because they knew we were hungry. Once I ate breakfast I went back to my tent and slept until I woke up in the afternoon.

When I woke up, I went down to the river to wash my face. After that I made a fire and waited for the ashes to break down. While that was happening, I went and got one of the turtles out from the bag and cut its throat. I moved the ashes and put the turtle in the middle laying on its belly. I covered it with the hot ashes, waited for about 30 minutes and then I turned the turtle on its back to let it cook for another 30 minutes. Once the turtle was cooked, I took it out of the hot ashes and put it on top of a cardboard box. I let it cool for ten minutes. While it was cooling down, I went and asked my big brother for a knife to crack it open. I then shared the turtle with my little brother and sister.

When we eat the turtle, we keep the meat in the shell and we also like to add salt to make it taste a bit more delicious. The best part of a turtle is the liver. It is good for you and very tasty.

We Are Inseparable

ED, 12 & DW, 13, Manyallaluk

Hi, we're Zeko and Dusty, and we're good mates from Manyallaluk. Manyallaluk is a small community where our family lives and where Glenda also lives. Glenda goes to boarding school with us in Nhulunbuy. Manyallaluk is roughly a one-to-two-hour drive from Katherine. But we don't get to Katherine often. We have lots of crazy stories about growing up in Manyallaluk. Most of our memories are from times spent with family out bush hunting. We want to share these stories with you.

Hi, I'm Zeko, I call Dusty's mum's sister, which makes Dusty my nephew. He calls me uncle. This is how we relate. We are both born in the same year and our birthdays are 14 days apart. We are inseparable. We go hunting and fishing together, camping, both went to the same primary school and are now both boarding at D̲awurr Boarding School. But we are quite different in personalities.

There are lots of great spots for hunting and fishing both

close to the community and long way away.

We love going hunting for cattle. For this we must go far away from the community and only men and boys go out hunting for cattle. One time we killed four cattle in one day with the four-wheeler Polaris, chasing them with it, bumping them and hitting them in the head to try and roll them. You see sometimes we don't need that whitefella tucka, when we get hungry we tell those boys let's go hunting for cattle, bullocky, kangaroo, and emu. We very rarely go into Katherine for whitefella tucka, only sometimes when we get money we go into Katherine. We mainly eat food off the land. When we get a big catch and have leftovers, we freeze it down to last us. One bullocky last us a month. When we do get a chance to go into Katherine we stock up on rice, flour, tea, and sugar. We get smart, we use the cattle fat as cooking oil. Make the oil hot then put beef in the pan. We love the wild bullocky, not that station beef.

When we are out hunting with our brothers, cousins, uncles, fathers and grandfathers they teach us everything we need to know. Zeko's brother taught us to cut up bullocky.

We also love drinking kangaroo blood it makes you strong and can make you jump higher. We drink the kangaroo blood as we are chopping up the kangaroo.

When it is rain season, we go looking for bush tucka. We love finding those bush apples.

We love going out camping, there are some great spots around our community. Wire Yard is our favourite spot for camping though. We must drive there and often we tow the buggy and two-wheeler out there. Down from Wire Yard is

Katherine River. We love this spot because we can go fishing, we go with our family and cruise around on the buggy and two-wheeler.

Hi, I'm Dusty, my favourite bush food to eat is bullocky and emu. Did you know the emu got its long neck because it got a stick in it? It's a story from long time ago. There was an old lady who put a stick in its neck to make it long and later changed herself into an emu. The emu tastes better than chicken. The fat of the emu we put it on our feet, rub it in to moisturise them.

One time, we went out hunting with bow and arrow, not far from the community, on the other side of the swamp. Those buffalo often come into our community. We shot a buffalo with the bow and arrow, I hit it right in the heart, it ran off and did a front flip. The arrow went further into the buffalo, killed it. We then cut it, feed the dogs the legs and we eat the rest, freezing for later. We cook the beef/buffalo in the frying pan and have it with rice and we love having it with homemade bread. We put yeast, flour and water together and put it in the oven, don't make too much noise, that homemade bread is like a baby, if you make noise it won't cook. If no noise the homemade bread will rise nice and high but if we make noise that homemade bread won't rise. So, the whole house goes quiet. We let it cook for an hour maybe.

This is us. This is our community and what we get up to.

We Are Similar

DG, 14, Nhulunbuy

My grandfather is strong, he works on our homeland all the time and he speaks good English. He helps our family, and his sons help him to clean the community. Everyone works together. My grandfather is important to me as well as all my family.

He is a worker that is loud and angry nearly all the time.

His favorite drink is sparkling water, and his favorite food is seafood like stingray, mud crab, and turtle.

He can't live without going out fishing on the boat and on foot. He taught me about fishing, and about helping the land. Grandparents are important because they know so much and can help others that come to our land.

My family's homeland is Blue Mud Bay in East Arnhem Land, Northern Territory. In the holidays my family and I travel back to Blue Mud Bay from Nhulunbuy. We drive about three hours along the dusty and bumpy red road, but the long drive is worth it. The drive is usually boring and relaxing and quiet. That's the time for me to go to sleep. Once we make it over the sand hills, we see the sparkling turquoise water and I feel home. I feel amazed and excited for all the wild adventures, hunting, fishing, dancing and stories we will share. This is the best time for us to connect and share our culture. My grandfather on my father's side shares our story. He is old; he is 96 years old and still makes jokes to make us laugh.

My family and I all go hunting for kangaroos, fish, dugongs, turtles and crabs. There will be my big brother, Josh, my mum, Lucille, and my nephew, Jezariah.

This one time we went hunting for big red boxing kangaroos with a crossbow near the beach in a clear field with a beautiful sunset. Kangaroos are easier to hunt with crossbow or a rifle. Sometimes we can bump with our truck. We caught five kangaroos that day. We cut the tails off and cooked them up on the fire to eat. The smell is strong, but the taste is good. The tail is hard to chew off the bone but worth the effort. Afterwards we walked on the beach along the blue crystal water. We walked and walked until we got to our big house near the airport, inland from the water. We slept 12 hours until the sun rose. We ate breakfast and I went to school and then went back home. Then me, my brother, uncle and the whole family went camping at the tower. When we slept, we heard a thump. We woke up and saw a little joey with his mother. We stayed there for a week and came back home, packed up our clothes and travelled back to Nhulunbuy.

Once we were back, we went to Yirrkala and then to Rocky Bay. We got my uncle's boat and drove to a little island called Sandy Beach. We stepped on the warm, white sand and we looked for some turtle tracks so we could find their eggs. We found three tracks and we paired off to dig the turtle nests. It took five minutes to dig all the eggs up to the surface while my mum, sister and my brother made some tents for us to sleep in. I helped my dad collect firewood and build a fire. We boiled them in a big pot of water on the fire, they are gooey and taste a little bit like chicken eggs. They are so good. We stay up late and even though it's been a tiring time I am happy from spending quality time with my friends and family.

My favorite part of my holiday is sitting

around the campfire and telling stories. All the adults share stories from a long time ago and the children listen.

Spending time with family is important to me because it's the time when we can pass our culture onto our kids or younger siblings so, when they grow up, they will pass on what they learned when they are adults and have babies. And hopefully this will happen for centuries to come. Repeating our culture and doing the same things that our ancestors did when they were alive – like going fishing, hunting and dancing every day – will make sure our culture just keeps going on and on. By 2030 my community will grow bigger and will have their own city or town.

My home is beautiful. Just like how my homeland is beautiful, you will love all the people who live there. These people will show you kindness and take you for a tour around the community. That's how we live our lives in this community.

I Felt Like a Mermaid As I Glided Swiftly Through the Fresh Water

EG, 15, Nhulunbuy

It was Saturday, the morning after our crazy Friday night party. I woke up to the sun shining through my window and onto my face. I struggled to open my eyes as I kicked my blanket off. We knew it was gonna be a hot day, so we decided to drive to Guwatjurumurru River to have a swim and keep cool.

Me and my sisters helped pack up the car with Mum and Dad, then made some lunch so we could get on the road.

Once we got on the dusty track and after we passed the airport and I put the music on, my little sisters fell asleep. Dad kept driving. Although I wanted to fall asleep too, I couldn't because it was too bumpy.

It was around 10 am in the morning when we left town and arrived at the river around 11 am. The water was a bit murky, and we were kind of scared to swim but Miwal (my youngest sister) wouldn't stop hassling us to get in the water. We grabbed a couple of big rocks from the ground and chucked them in the rockpool to see if it was safe to swim because that's what Dad normally does. It looked safe enough, so we all walked down to the water and jumped in. Our dog Max followed. I was the first out of my sisters to get in. I felt like a mermaid as I glided swiftly through the fresh water. My sisters followed. Mum and Dad were still at the top camp area drinking tea and eating biscuits by the fire.

After maybe 25 to 30 minutes, we hopped out of the water and went up to camp to get some food because we were starving. We walked up the trail to get to the back of the car.

While Gungulma, Warani and I grabbed the mat to sit on and eat lunch, Miwal got the food out of the camping fridge. Mum and Dad got the drinks out of the Esky for us. We sat down all together to eat our food and enjoy the beauty of mother nature. Suddenly, we all got a sick feeling and something felt off. We looked at each other like we knew something was missing.

"MAX! Where's Max?" yelled Miwal.

We dropped our lunches and rushed back down to the water.

"You two go that way and me and Warani will go this way," I said.

Warani lead the way across the waterfall and onto the other side of the river. We followed a bush path that wound around the cliff, screaming his name and whistling like crazy.

We could hear Gungulma and Miwal from the top of the cliff still looking everywhere for Max. It was nearly the time where we'd have to start to pack up and head home, but we couldn't go home without him.

Warani and I were tired and getting ready to walk back to camp and meet up with Gungulma and Miwal. Five minutes passed and we decided to turn back. While we were walking back through the eucalyptus trees and dodging the prickles of the gunga (pandanus) leaves, we started to think maybe something could have got Max. Warani thought that maybe Max stayed in the water and a crocodile came up behind him and dragged him underneath. I didn't want to believe something like that had happened, not to Max. He wasn't like that, he knew when it wasn't safe to stay somewhere, he knew he had to stay close to us.

We walked down the cliff onto the bush path and back through the rockpools. We found Gungulma and Miwal sitting in the pools looking just as worried as us. I walked across the rocks, Warani alongside me. We sat down altogether in silence for a bit until Gungulma asked if we could go back up to camp, and think about what we should do about Max.

We walked up the trail together and reached the top. We went to fold the mat back up until we heard a fast-panting noise coming from behind the car. Miwal ran over to where the noise was coming from. She bent down and poked her head around the corner with a relieved look on her face. Guess who was lying down in a big puddle in front of the car?

It was Max!

We hopped in the car and put Max in the backseat, excited to get home and tell our big brothers about the crazy and adventurous day we had.

My Grandfather

SL, 14, Ramingining

When I was four years old my grandfather left all the families from Ramingining. He wanted to go and travel all around the communities with his friends and other family members who also wanted to act with my grandfather. He went to Adelaide to stay there with his wife, Mary, who is our grandmother. He started to become a very brave old man because he was helping other people from different places. He stayed in Adelaide for couple of years with Nana Mary and when he started to go and act with his old friends he remembered all the memories from his homeland and he said to himself, "I want to make all my families proud." He wanted to go back and help his community in Ramingining.

When he used to stay at Ramingining it was bushy and there were too many kids and other families. Every time we would go for afternoon walk with families and friends we would always go to our favourite spot where our nana always sat down and did weaving with pandanus. She would make baskets and earrings with our sisters Charmaine, Jasmine, Rowena and Tyrene. When we go for walk, we also would go to the shop and get some food and snacks for our picnic.

Every Thursday there's a basketball competition for all the kids at Ramingining. Me and my sisters dress up in our favourite jerseys and we go to the basketball court near the school and we play against the boys or different teams.

When Grandpa was 18 years old, he went to Maningrida to go to school there with other families and friends. He shared his culture with them so they knew where he was from and what clan he was from. They knew what family he was from, where he lived and stayed and what he wanted to do when he grew up. He went on to do acting, singing, dancing and sharing his culture with other people so they can pass it down to their new generation.

When Grandpa got sick with cancer, he was worried. He couldn't standup from sleep. He got sick and weak; he couldn't eat anything or go for walk with Nana Mary when he was like that. All the family from Ramingining and Gupulul, they kept on calling him and kept on checking if he was alright.

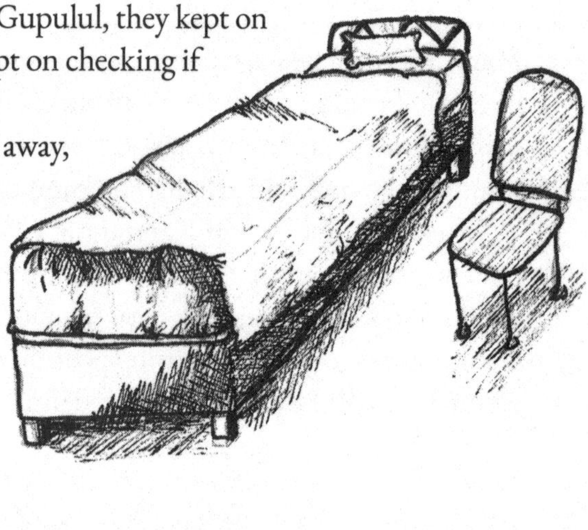

When he passed away, that night Nana Mary was crying and worried because she had no husband to look after her and stay with her. The people from Adelaide hospital called my family to let us know that Grandpa passed away. All the families were crying really loudly. They miss Grandpa very much. The next day we went to the house they told me about my grandpa and I heard them say, "Oh, Samantha's grandpa passed away yesterday in the middle of the night." I was crying and crying really hard.

He was rightfully proud. He wanted his storytelling through film to be shared, to be on the record for the generations to come.

We Saw Bubbles In the Water

SD, 14, Ramingining

One sunny day, I was at home in Ramingining (Ramo) with my nana Mary (Dhapalany), my mum Valarie (Nawali) and my cousin Carmain. I remember my nana asked all of us to go hunting with her, as she wanted to find file snake (bulokminy) – she loves hunting for file snake because it is her favourite bush food to eat. Nana wanted to find bush food and to tell us stories about how she finds file snake.

I can remember Nana went to my school to let the principal know that she was going to take us girls out hunting in the bush. I felt excited for her to take us to eat bush food. It is a special time with my family. Sharing food we have caught ourselves and hunting together.

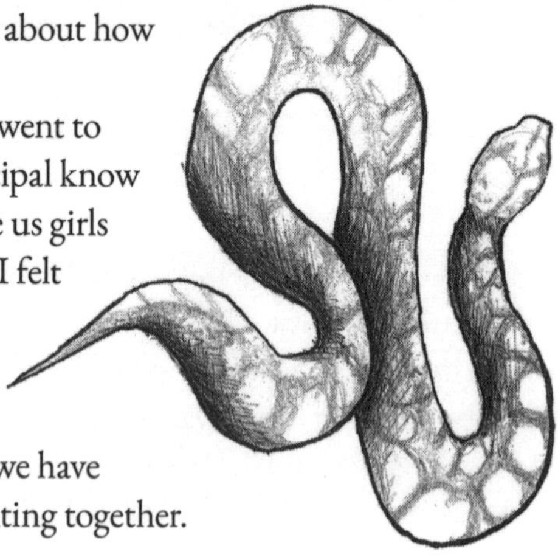

We went into the bush. It takes about an hour to walk from my home to the creek. There are lots of pandanus trees in the bushland. There are also lots of bush plums and bush apples. They are up high in the trees and we throw rocks at them to get them down! We saw cockatoos in the trees.

My mum stayed back to make fire with Carmain in a clearing in the dirt. I walked with my two nanas (Evonne and Mary) to the other side past a big log towards the creek. Bright green water trees follow the creek all the way to my grandfather's house. We sometimes go there for funeral or to visit family.

When we got to the creek, we saw bubbles in the water. I knew that was a file snake because Nana had taught me other times. I put my hand into the water to feel around to find the snake's head and then I grabbed it. I put it in the bag.

Nana said, "Good girl, Sabina!"

We caught five more file snakes that day. My nanas are the best at catching them and always catch the most file snakes.

After we catch file snake we either cook it in the bush or take it home for my family. We cook it on the fire and once it is cooked we peel the skin off the snake. We eat the meat and any eggs inside the snake. The meat tastes like fish. I really like the taste of file snake!

On our way back to the clearing we saw a big buffalo (detun) lying next to the creek. The buffalo had a big scar on its neck. The buffalo couldn't walk. My nanas told me the mark on its neck was from a crocodile (baru) that had attacked. We saw the baru slide going into the creek in the sand.

I love spending time with my nanas. My nanas teach us how to weave with pandanus leaves. Nana Mary is so good at weaving. When we weave, we find a pandanus tree, we chop the leaves down with a hook. To colour the leaves we dig up different tree roots from under a tree, boil them and put the leaves in. The different roots make the leaves change to the different colours we need. I weave yapa mats, earrings, bracelets and baskets. Sometimes it takes a long time and my hands cramp.

I also do lots of dancing at ceremonies. My nanas are really good at dancing, they teach me. I dance with my mum and my nanas in Ramo. I like to dance because there is lot of people there watching and dancing together.

A favourite memory I have is cooking for Nana Mary. She wanted me to make her breakfast. I made her weetbix and a tea with milk and sugar. She said, "Thank you my beautiful girl."

The most important lesson Nana has taught me is to do my best. She tells me I need to focus on my culture.

I always listen to her. Sometimes. She tells me off when I don't.

"Listen to me because I'm your nana."

Family Is More Important Than My Life

BF, 17, Warruwi

Wind. People talking. Loud music.

It's my grandma's house, so there are fences and there's the bush and plants and trees. Then there is the beach right next door.

When I walk in the front door, I can see plenty of plates and my mum cooking something with my grandma. When I walk in my room, I can see that it is clean. My room is cold. When I walk outside, I can see my grandma and my sister and mother, and I sit with them. Spending time with family is important to me.

Mum, she's the same size as me and she reminds me all the

time to look after her. She is always laughing and has a funny face. She loves me and cares about me. My mother also taught me how to practice my culture by teaching me dancing, cooking, and how to look after my brothers and sisters and nephews, and myself when I get older. She lives in Darwin now to help my sister with her new baby.

Uncle George, he is a bit taller and bigger than me. He loves fishing and his family. My uncle taught me how to drive the boat. He is a good teacher because he is thoughtful. He is also patient. He takes me fishing sometimes.

Aunty Rhonda, she also lives in Warrawi. She cooks turtle and it tastes good. We will soon be all together in Darwin for Christmas. To be together makes me happy. Every time I sleep over at Uncle's house, my aunty is good and kind.

Ama (Grandma) lives alone in Darwin, but we visit her. She makes damper, and it's "GOOOOD!" She is very lonely, so my mum asked my family to visit to her house in Darwin while mum and I were in Goulburn to make her feel happy and better (:

Brother Russell, he looks like me but is much taller and he acts normal and sometimes laughs. He loves basketball and fishing. I like playing basketball with him. He beats me all the time. I go hunting with my brother and my sister and I went to camping with them for a night. We went camping when it was windy. There is an ocean there. I smell ocean, great looking fish and wind. I see the nature, ocean, turtle egg and fish. I touch the fish for the first time and turtle egg for the first time, it tasted delicious and fantastic.

Sister Miriam, she is the same size as me. She loves her son,

Torres, and her family. She helps him to do his homework. She also helps him to clean his room. During the holidays, I spend time with my sister and nephew. We go shopping and buy chocolate biscuits and soft drinks. My sister has moved to Darwin. I miss her, but I get to fly to Darwin to see her newborn baby in three weeks. She had another boy, named Ezekeil. During last holidays, I was staying at home and called Darwin on the phone all day and all night from 10 pm to 8 am. I do this every time, I'm on break. I sometimes go outside but. Walking with my mum and my big sister sometimes for fresh air and shopping has made me feel happy and better.

Then there's me Brian. Every time my mum sees me on my school break she is so happy and all my family in Darwin are so happy and hug me. I can talk sometimes but I must get it out my chest so I can talk to people and my family.

When We Went to a Creek Named Devils

LB, 16, Warruwi

The day I started Trinity Bay State High School was February 3rd, 2021. I was a 13-year-old girl in Year 8 and was shy when I went to my classes because that was my first time starting that school. The next day when I went to school, I had assembly for Year 8. When I was in there, that was the first time I met two of my best friends and their names were Preston & Kalila, but Preston was the one that hanged with me all the time.

My best memories of him were basically everything, we did everything together. Every day after school me, Preston and my other friends we walked to the library at Raintree Shopping Centre located at Manunda, Cairns. Me, Preston and others of my friends we sometimes went to Cairns Central and The Esplanade just to walk around and if we had bucks, we'd go buy food, jewellery or clothes.

My best memory of Preston is when we went to a creek named Devils. My other friends were there too. We had a sleepover that day and we were bored and wanted to go out because it was hot like boiling lava. We'd always catch the bus because Devils is on the other side, it's a really a long walk but like a ten-minute bus ride from my friend Nayila's house to Redlynch.

Preston is important to me. He's always been there for me. I was always following him around, he would message me more than my other friends. Preston always cared about me, even when I was feeling down. He always came to hug me, to see if I was alright. We do everything together.

A Good Day For Boating

SG, 18, Warruwi

In Warruwi (my community), I remember the island is surrounded by water, sandy beaches and gum trees. It feels peaceful, quiet and safe. My home is full of family, including Uncle, Grandad, Grandma, Mum, Nanna, cousins, brothers and sisters; it is always busy, but I like it.

Any day is a good day for boating in Warruwi. I would go fishing in the boat with my family. We would venture from South Goulburn to North Goulburn in our boat, a small tinny with a 60HP motor. We used handlines to catch GTs, queenies and coral trout. From the boat we could see dugongs, turtles, sharks and reef.

Day or night I could go turtle hunting with my uncle around North Goulburn. I remember going

out hunting for the first time. I was eight years old when my uncle told me that he was going hunting. I asked him if I could come along, he grumbled, "Yeah, let's go." My uncle is funny, a good talker and has great stories. He drinks a little too much, but he is really important to me.

The boat trip is always bumpy because the tinny has low sides. I could taste the salt in the air and smell the fuel from the motor. That trip, we caught a turtle with a long harpoon but we had to chase the turtle then spear it. We took it home, cracked the head, sliced the neck, took the guts, the liver and the heart out. We used hot rocks inside the turtle and then we put the leaves in the neck cavity. Then we put the turtle on its back on the fire. We build another fire on its belly. Then, we wait until the fire cools down.

A Good Future For Me

DY, 15, Yirrkala

Art

The special moment happened when I was at her house. That was next to Yirrkala beach. On that special day, it was rainy and windy. The clouds were closing around the sun like they do usually on a rainy day.

My dad was in his room sitting on the floor. The lino cutter was beneath his feet and his artwork unfinished. He was only cutting half the page and the other half of the page was empty. Back then he would draw on one side of the page, cut the lino and repeat the step for the other page. One half would take him one hour.

I rushed in and I sat next to him. I was wondering if I could draw too. He was having a break drinking his coffee. I asked him.

"You can if you practise a lot," he said.

So as my father did his drawing, I got my own empty page and started to draw too. This was my first drawing. Most of the time I wasn't practising, I was fidgeting. I was just nine at the time and didn't know what I was doing.

Imagination is something that you can put on a piece of paper. Sometimes I would draw things I saw in movies. Sometimes I would draw things I saw off an image. Sometimes I would sit down with the friends I have around me. I would freeze in the spot and in between the relaxation I would spot a tree or clouds making shapes and imagine it transforming into another image. Suddenly, a car with a dent would have a face or a tree would have an expression. In that process, I would get the things I would usually use to draw: a pencil, a pen, a rubber, a ruler. The thing that all artists would use for their drawings is a book. I feel relaxed when I start imagining what that thing is in the sky or on the tree. Drawing is a way to calm me down in every scenario. Especially when I don't want to go to class, feel down or when other people around me are being too loud.

The people that influenced me were with me in the days of my childhood and they are the people I dearly love. So, as one of these people I dearly love passed away, I promised to be an artist. That was two years ago and, on that day, when she passed away, I promised that I would take her industry as the artist she wanted me to be. I don't know what it means to take her industry as an artist. Until I do, I'll have to finish school and discover my artistic style.

The things I did with my grandma I can't describe but I remember the happy feeling of being with her. I don't remember everything, but she did a good amount of things and I thank her for that. My grandma did lots of paperbark paintings. Always really big paintings. She would give them to people and the arts centre at Yirrkala. I have not many words that I can use to describe her and the things I've done with her, but I do have the memories with her and they were the best. I'll not forget about them. All my memories are special, and I will not tell anyone because they're my only memories.

I think it's time for new generations to open up their own ideas and to create their own careers with the help of past artists.

Trust

Bernie and Ricky are the two teachers that help us within Clontarf. They're like mentors. Most Clontarf lessons are health with Miwatj. They help us to get jobs and get bank cards. Whenever we are not in classes, Ricky and Bernie always encourage us to go to our classes. I listen to them because of the way that they respect us; they respect us more than any teacher. At the start of school, before we came to high school, every Wednesday and Friday they would take us to the Clontarf room and talk about the things we have in common and the things that we love to do. After many years, they gained our trust. It takes years to gain other people's trust. Whenever we are down, they allow us to come to Clontarf and hang out with them.

Bernie and Ricky see a good future for me, and they see many good futures for others. They give us confidence. Whenever we have to go somewhere where we don't want to go, they talk about their personal experiences. They help us get over our fears and teach us to push through the fear.

The best memory I have with Ricky and Bernie is ... well there are so many memories up in my head and none are the best. But there is one. Here in boarding the Clontarf boys and the Yirrkala Clontarf boys were sitting in the middle on the concrete seat in the middle of the boarding house. Bernie and Sam were giving some awards to some of the boys, and I was one of these boys. I was not expecting to get an award. They gave me a woomera and I was happy because it felt good and I was proud.

Memory

One year ago, my family and I were driving our near East Woody. East Woody isn't that far, it's close to Nhulunbuy where I live. Halfway there, my dad spotted a few buffalos behind the fence. There were three of them and then I realised that they were a family. A dad, a mum, and the son or daughter.

Solitude

I'm addicted to fishing and well-known for my fishing. The places where I do fishing in Nhulunbuy are at East Woody and Daliwuy Bay. I also go to Bawaka. This place is my dad's home but it's not the only place he calls home. Bawaka is very calm, but it is also very dangerous with it being with full of crocodiles, sharks, stingrays and box jellyfish.

Fishing makes me feel like me. Fishing is somewhat how you release all your anger. If I have problems back at home, the thing that goes through my mind is to go out and release that anger. Then, when I go back home, I am much calmer than I was before I went fishing. It's a hobby where most times you catch and lose, but that is a part of how things go. Sometimes you may catch giant fish, sometimes you may catch nothing. Even if you do catch something, it's very stress free. The main thing that goes through my mind when I am casting is whether there are some fish chasing my lure. There's always life hanging around.

I go fishing with my dad and brothers and sometimes I go fishing by myself. It's when you have your own time of relaxation. The difference is that it's a bit more stressful when you go with other people and they are using your fishing gear.

Solitude is important to me because it's self-relaxing and keeps me away from worries at home.

The Nationals

RY, 13, Yirrkala

In 2022, I got picked to represent the East Arnhem Region and do athletics in Darwin. In each event I would get really excited and nervous at the same time. I came second in javelin, the 400m race, the 200m race and the 100m race. In 2022, I didn't get picked for the nationals, but when I went back and did it again in 2023, I got picked to go the nationals in Tasmania.

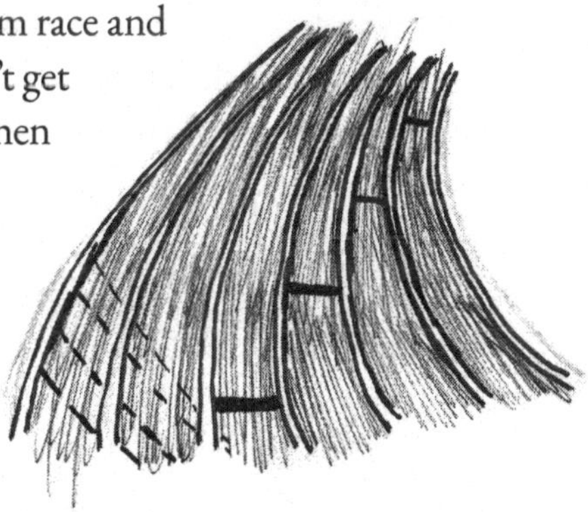

When I went back to the stadium in Darwin and did my 400m race, I improved big time. I got a new PB. In Tasmania, I also got a new PB for my 200m race and my 100m race.

In the Marara Stadium in Darwin, while the others in my team were still completing, I signed out with my parents to go to the Casuarina Shopping Centre. I went into the shop with my parents and they got me some new clothing and did food shopping and we were in there for like an hour and a half. Then we went back to the stadium so I could compete. The next day I got ready and had breakfast with the other students in my team. We got on the bus and drove to the stadium. When one of my teammates was on the track racing I was cheering for them because I had finished all my events. I was cheering for them from the side lines.

In the night, we went out for dinner at the wharf and we had lots of delicious food. The next day we got up early in the morning and we had to get ready, have breakfast and go to the airport so we could head back home. When me and my team got back to the airport, my mum was there waiting for me to give me my new clothes and to say goodbye to me. After that, we went up to the check in and then we bought some snacks for the flight back. Then, our coach told us to get our medals out to take some pictures from some of our events.

When I got back home, I was so excited to see my fam bam and friends. I was most excited to see my grandma, Rarriwuy Marika. After all of that, I had to rep NT in Tasmania with a few girls that I raced back in Darwin.

Acknowledgements

This book is the product of almost two years of dedication. Students worked hard to produce the stories, and teachers and mentors worked hard to support them. The collection wouldn't have been made without the contributions of a wonderful group of people. Thank you to the parents and families of Dawurr students. Thank you to everyone who helped the students craft their stories: Amy White, Amy Nichols, Deanna Trembath, Lee Gordon, Ella Martin, Erin Martin, James Hammond, Meg Kent-Spark, Brett Osbourne, Darcy Walsh, Rhoda Shine, Daniel Lewinski, Anthea Lewinski, Steph Gorman, Jeff Horoch, Rachel Millard, Harry McCallum, Swahnnya De Almeida, Groover and Kylie Mercer. Ethan Jolley worked particularly hard in the final month to ensure that this would reach the printers before Christmas. Ash French and Gemma Totterdell supported Daydae as he completed the illustrations for the book and threw up their hands to help out at many different stages of the writing process.

Everything good that happens at Dawurr is in large part the fault of Kiri Deegan.

Daydae Yunupingu, one of our incredibly talented students, created the artwork for the book. This illustration is of his renowned grandmother and his inspiration, the late Dr B Marika AO.

Thank you, Oli

We just want to take a moment to acknowledge senior teacher Oliver Friedmann. His vision and hard work in bringing this book to life is nothing short of amazing. Oli knows how important it is for young people to tell their stories, and you can feel his belief in the D̲awurr boarders on every single page. We are forever grateful for Oli's dedication to the D̲awurr Boarders and ensuring their stories are heard and their communities are proud. But nothing says this more than the words of the students themselves...

Kiri Deegan, Deputy Head of Boarding

Oli, we the kids thank you for doing the book with us. You've done hard work putting this all together. It makes us share our story to the people we want to. And we truly thank you for doing a project to show the boarding kids that you can do big things with just a little effort and the help of your teacher and friends. We can't imagine doing this without you. You encouraged us to use our own words, and helped us with spelling and typing on the computer. You were kind, helpful and honest. You made this so we can show what we've done in our life and tell our homeland. You worked deeply and strongly hard for the book to be continued during tutoring times without you at boarding. You are passionate and kind with a heart, always helping with a smile and proudness. You're a great dude. A very funky teacher and a really cool and kind gentleman.

We all thank you, Oli.

About D̲awurr Boarding

D̲awurr Boarding is a 40-bed co-ed boarding facility located on Rirratjingu land in Nhulunbuy, North East Arnhem Land. Established in 2017, D̲awurr supports students from across the Northern Territory in accessing quality education and wellbeing programs, while remaining close to culture, Country and communities.

D̲awurr is a safe and welcoming community where open communication and discussion with families and community members is essential. We value their input regarding the welfare and cultural needs of their children. By involving family and community members in the decision-making process, we enhance the overall experience for our boarders while ensuring we are aligned with cultural expectations.

We take pride in our students, who thrive in this home away from home. They share the joys of trying new things, building lasting friendships, and navigating challenges with maturity and resilience. At D̲awurr, we focus on the whole person, celebrating each student's journey and contributions to our unique community.

About the Indigenous Literacy Foundation

The Indigenous Literacy Foundation (ILF) is a national charity working with Aboriginal and Torres Strait Islander remote Communities across Australia. We are Community-led, responding to requests from remote Communities for culturally relevant books, including early learning board books, resources, and programs to support Communities to create and publish their stories in languages of their choice.

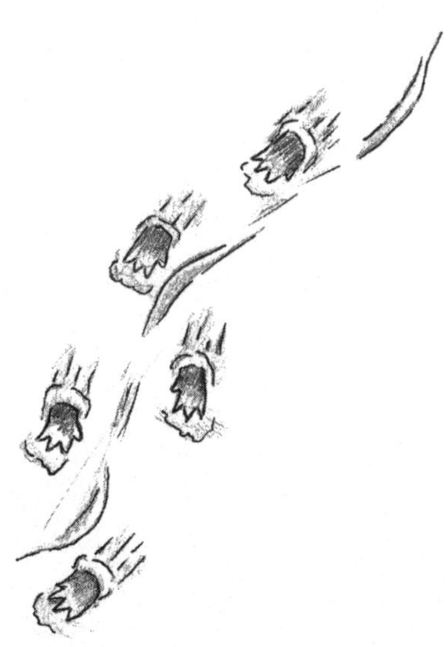